ZERO DEFECT OLIVE OILS

QA planning for the protected designation of origin

Salvatore Fiore

This publication is designed to provide accurate and authoritative information in regard to the subject matter covered. It is sold with the understanding that the publisher is not engaged in rendering legal, accounting, or other professional service. If legal advice or other expert assistance is required, the services of a competent professional person should be sought.

Salvatore Fiore

Zero defect olive oils: QA planning for the protected designation of origin.

© 2017 Salvatore Fiore. All rights reserved.

ISBN 9781976749667

This publication may not be reproduced, stored in a retrieval system, or transmitted in whole or in part, in any form or by any means, electronic, mechanical, photocopying, recording, or otherwise, without the prior written permission of the author. The scanning, uploading, or distribution of this book via the Internet or any other means without the express permission of the author is illegal and punishable by law. Please purchase only authorized editions of this work and do not participate in or encourage piracy of printed copyrighted materials, electronically or otherwise. Your support of the author's rights is appreciated. The author can be contacted at **contact@salvatorefiore.com**

To my mother and my father, they taught me how windy and cold days won't stop harvesting, and for my olive oil trainers, lecturers and professors as without them I would have never made it.

Salvatore Fiore

Carosino, 15th December 2017

Contents

Foreword, 7

Introduction, 9

Value chain, 11

Porter's value chain, 16

Supply chain, 17

Added value, 19

The quality process, 22

Quality assurance strategy, 25

Zero defect philosophy, 28

Intangible qualities, 31

Quantifying intangibility, 34

Traceability as differentiation, 37

Zero defect management, 40

The meaning of quality, 45

Considerations, 49

Bibliography, 53

Abouth the author, 57

Foreword

I decided to write this book after receiving many useful suggestions by colleagues involved in management, education and production of high quality olive oils. In fact there aren't in circulation many books that examine the Protected Designation of Origin olive oil industry, due mainly to the complex workings of the supply chain, the slow entrance in the large distribution and a sceptical market. There was a need to fill this gap and I decided to make some of my academic writings available in this book. They request some understanding and familiarity with strategy, administration and marketing, although the more experienced reader will have no difficulty in going through the pages.

In the book I explain, step by step, how the Protected Designation of Origin olive oil industry works and how to define your place within the supply chain with low cost activities as a strategic choice for the future market of high quality olive oils. Purposefully I have taken the Protected Designation of Origin olive oil "Terra di Bari" as an example case study and after a careful analysis I generalize it as a valid model for other supply chains with interesting and down-to-earth future prospects. I also illustrate some strategies to integrate smoothly within the supply chain satisfying consumer demands. In reality I also thought useful to leave a note for all the colleagues who would like to embark on Protected Designation of Origin olive oil production as other production channels become saturated by imports, whilst there are some signals of the market stagnating.

As growth is slowed down by the maturation of some Extra Virgin olive oils, some may find my methodology an interesting option. Finally, I have began to think on how to integrate production for the higher end market within segments defined by consumers educated to high standard of taste and flavour. Purposefully I report some useful insights for not being left behind by a market in continuous evolution.

Salvatore Fiore

Introduction

In recent times sales of olive oils have been gaining momentum due to interest from various countries. Appreciation for the Mediterranean diet, has boosted export from countries producing olive oils towards countries previously accustomed to the use of other fatty acids and in particular those of animal origin.

Olive oil has a major role in the diet of Italians and over time, the consumption of olive oil has generated a substantial industry that has seen a steady economic progression. The Italian olive oil industry is well structured on a large scale and is present throughout south Italy, where olive oil production is an important part of the local economy. The Italian olive growing industry, although very well developed, is undergoing a restructuring in order to compete on the international market with the objective of integrating the supply chain within the diverse entrepreneurship present in various regions. The main objective of this restructuring is to achieve international excellence in the production of standard and upmarket olive oils, differentiated by a variety of nutritional characteristics, enhancing the oil quality.

The EU regulates the market with laws in which descriptions and definitions of olive oils and their chemical characteristics are fixed. Producers, transformers and distributors are free to excess the already stringent standards of the European Union or to contribute with research.

Current research into olive growing is focussing on modernisation and intensification of specialized plantations and development of innovative techniques of analysis for quality enhancement. Most olive oil chemical analyses are focused towards the identification of standard parameters through which it is possible to discern qualities. In cases of fraud such as the blending of lower quality oils, chemical analyses can help to mitigate the likely impact on human consumption and help to reduce counterfeiting. Modern consumers of olive oil are health conscious and very well informed on the benefits of genuine olive oils. Purchasing by consumers is now likely to be based as much on the medical properties of oils, as on preference of taste and flavour or other sensory characteristics. Such properties are therefore important purchase decision factors which can be essential for consumers with medical conditions.

Value chain

There exist many types of olive oil for human consumption, as defined by EU regulations. Consumer choices are dependent upon price or other factors relating to health, taste and flavour preferences, branding or convenience. The most common types of olive oil found nowadays on trade are all edible, as defined by law, but differ in quality and price.

Qualities of olive oil are an interesting focus for academic discussion, given that health benefits demonstrated by research to be associated with particular properties of olive oils are positively associated with taste and flavour appreciation by consumers, perceiving differences in qualities, which in turn reflect on prices. Product differentiation is one key to the production of high quality olive oil and this is simply done by adding value in the supply chain. The production of high quality olive oil is not a competitive advantage anymore for those regions which have previously produced low quality oil and subsequently have responded to high market demands by adjusting production accordingly. In fact demand from other countries of high quality Italian olive oils is increasing. Along this growth, there is also market demand for olive oils with unique characteristics not found in other types. In this sense Protected Designation of Origin olive oils (Designated olive oils) present an opportunity for product differentiation to increase shares in the high quality olive oil market. During cycles of economic crisis, producers are invited to differentiate their product, in order to stimulate demands that can beat economies of scale or stagnations created by the inability to cope with market demands. Last economic crisis has brought olive oil production prices down, as a consequence there has been lack of response to satisfy high demand for quality olive oils due to the very low profit margin left for the producers. Opening new niche areas in the market through product differentiation may alleviate some problems raised by market saturation.

Designated olive oils have been recently attracting significant interest as they present the customer with the opportunity to acquire a high quality product but most importantly to purchase attributes not present in other oils. The difference in price is not being regulated in any sense, differentiating the choice from the mainstream offered on the market. Such differentiation rests on providing added value attributed to the environment, weather and ground characteristics of the place where the oil originates.

The unique attributes characterizing the Protected Designation of

Origin olive oil in their flavours and qualities, are embedded in the product along with less tangible perceptions. Intangible qualities are attributes of the oil and include the culture of the place of origin, perceptions and values like the image of the territory of origin, food safety, traditions and their histories, all of which contribute to the final product. Such attributes differ from those correlated to physical properties which can be directly measured in laboratories and by expert review and are valued instead by the supply chain and the community of consumers as a whole.

Typical agricultural companies that are vertically integrated within the supply chain are in a position to contain labour and service costs for production and bottling of Designated olive oils. They are therefore best placed to seek a competitive advantage with product differentiation as the production falls within their control. Services for marketing and branding are needed in order to enhance and differentiate oil quality perceptions as added value for the supply chain and they are most probably sought for within external companies, as they require specialisation and market intelligence.

Educational developments should be sought by promoting training for new production processes and quality continuous improvement. Consumer education to taste and flavour and knowledge of Protected Designation of Origin olive oil qualities (tangible and intangible) are an integral part of such educational developments needed to complete the whole cycle from production to the experiential stage of consumption. Particularly consumer education is an interesting subject area to be explored alongside the meaning that training holds for supply chain employees and independent olive oil producers and the tension raised between working, learning and innovating. This conceptual shift requires to view all of them working together and not as separate activities manageable by single actors on the supply chain.

The olive oil supply chain structure, has been for a long time subject to transformation due to changes in production, qualities of oils and market demands. The political approach adopted by the industry has been one of leaving the supply chain to self-organise around market demands and legislation. In this way, whilst EU legislation have pulled the market, introducing new standards, supply chains have adapted passively to new market demands. Recent rationalizations and integrations with other agricultural supply chains have been characterized by price competition, sudden rise in export and market demands for high quality oils at affordable prices. This new trend has forced operators to reshape much of the supply chain around strategies of quality, product differentiation and price leadership. In fact, lack of appreciation by oil consumers, has been the main problem for the commercialisation of Designated oils.

These olive oils channel themselves naturally into strategies of product differentiation. It's no accident that its transformation process is differentiated from other types of processes of olive oil production. The Designated oil "Terra di Bari" is an example case study taken here to illustrate practically the functioning of the supply chain considering the Porter's value chain model and hence the investigation of what this means to supply chain participants.

Porter's value chain

The value chain of Michael Porter is a tool of analysis used to identify various activities in an organization in order to run them at an optimum level and gain competitive advantage, or to direct organizational strategies towards prefixed objectives. Activities in an organization should run efficiently and the cost of running them should not exceed their actual value. The basic principle is to identify the activities called primary and to separate them from the support. Primary activities are concerned with organization of input materials/information to be transformed. There are also activities of logistic post transformation and activities of marketing of products, after sale support and service. Support activities instead, use technology and information to create intelligence targeted at the optimisation of primary activities. Organizational strategy objectives are as such achieved when activities like procurement, technology, human resources development management and firm infrastructure, assist primary activities and the whole chain to work together in creating a superior competitive advantage, adding value to well performed activities.

Supply chain

The transformation process of olive into oil generally starts with inbound logistics. Olives from producers are transported to the transformation plant and stocked waiting to be pressed. This time bound activity is generally carried out within the same premises. Alternatively, olive producers sell their olives to transformers after careful tracking and recording of the plantation of origin. After transformation, the oil is stocked in containers for filtering and bottled on the same line or transported to distribution/bottling centres. Distribution centres bottle the oil, record the activities on tracking systems and make it available for sale or for integration within other agricultural product supply systems. The bottled oil is then transported to destination for sale or to other distribution centres for buffering of large grocery chain distributors. Customer service follows to inform clients on purchases made or educate on taste and flavour using feedback to inform marketing on customer complaints, preferences, tastes and any other information available for market intelligence. Protected Designation of Origin olive oil production and bottling are activities regulated and controlled by appropriate bodies authorised by the EU and governed by national and regional laws.

The Provincial Chamber of Commerce supervises and authorizes the Protected Designation of Origin logo and branding after accurate checks, chemical analysis and paperwork controls. Accurate checks with regard to the origin of olives and the type of plantation should be regularly certified to disciplinary standards and checked yearly to avoid major changes affecting the quality of olives. After cropping, olives are pressed in authorized pressing service companies and the transformation in oil is registered on special recording systems to facilitate traceability and certification of origin. The oil traced with certified olives is then bottled by the same pressing service system or sent to distributors for packaging after authorization by the chamber of commerce, obtaining the final Protected Designation of Origin status. All the activities spanning from cropping to bottling and distribution are governed by strict quality assurance procedures and are time critical in order to preserve intact the positive characteristics of the Designated oil. It is precisely the correct execution of this sequence of primary activities that guarantees the differentiation of Protected Designation of Origin olive oils from others which do not have comparable characteristics.

Added value

The Protected Designation of Origin olive oil supply chain is more expensive to run than other types due to the fact that all activities must be certified by recognized bodies authorised by law. Certifications are issued in order to protect consumers, avoid adulteration, counterfeiting and protect public health. The extra overhead incurred by the supply chain add to the final price.

Moreover, the olives price before transformation is penalized if compared to other non Designated olives due to higher costs of maintenance for the certified plantations. High quality olive oil starts with high quality of the fruits themselves. The traceability of the product on the supply chain has added costs for quality assurance also, administrations and maintenance of the supply chain itself. Such costs can be absorbed if activities and chain structure are optimized.

The quality assurance on the supply chain takes other variable costs added due to the fact that the final product is not a standardized piece of manufacturing plant but subject to changes arising from uncontrollable factors like changes in climate and other natural events. The olives are therefore subject to environmental conditions which can negatively influence the final product. Protected Designation of Origin olive oils have fixed characteristics of taste, flavour and chemical compositions as determined by the disciplinary EU law and adjustments or other type of product manipulation or alterations are not allowed. Information regarding olive characteristics is thus crucial before it reaches the pressing stage and the same can be said regarding the transformation process (olive stocking and pressing) which can be adjusted in order to guarantee the correspondence of the oil within the limits established by the disciplinary.

Research can be invaluable to inform the activities of plantation maintenance, harvesting and transformation on a yearly cyclic basis, as these are the most critical points of variability in the chain. However it should be emphasized that Protected Designation of Origin olive oils cannot be adapted for particular markets or customized to specific consumer demands. Consequently, the market has to be created in order to appreciate the characteristics of the oils as they are.

The value chain is however managed within a larger system, coupling to a larger flow of activities in a value system. Many firms (producers, transformers, distributors) concur and it is precisely amongst those firms that information must be shared. Strategies and vision can be shared through the supply chains involved in the value system.

The key factor to the success of the value chain is the flow of the right information through the activities and the decision process informing job-roles on the actions to be taken throughout the supply chain. The shorter the supply chain the higher the added value for olive producers. The chain is said to be "short" when the activities are carried out by few firms and are located in proximity to each other.

The quality process

The EU fixes supply chain standards for Protected Designation of Origin products in order to guarantee products originality and the geographical connections that come with it for consumers to enjoy. The organization and the structure that the supply chain gives itself are not regulated by the EU like other activities on the chain. However the prescribed outcomes are fixed and must be met at each single check point on the chain and records are kept for each action that can influence subsequent activities as contained within EU regulation CEE 2081/92.

The assumptions made by the EU quality assurance is that self-organisation of the supply chain can increment efficiency and fit most of the situations if law regulates the main procedures and activities. Moreover checks are made by certified authorities to protect the quality trade mark attributed to the product with characteristics which are unique to the territory in which it is produced. The whole cycle of production of a Protected Designation of Origin olive oil has to be carried out in a predefined geographically delimited area as reported within the disciplinary text and cannot be reproduced outside it. In order to gain a Designated trade mark however there should be two conditions to satisfy article 2 of regulation CEE 2081/92. More precisely, article 2 requires that the characteristics of a product are as they are due to the geographical and human factors and at the same time the production of raw materials and their transformations into a product should be done in the same region as the finished product which bears the Designated trade/mark. Quality control procedures identify the production Designated areas, the conditions of production, the natural characteristics of the environment, the variety of oils, the type of plantation and cultivations, the maximum production of olives per hectare and the type of transformation process. Importantly for the final phase, it is the list of all the chemical-physical characteristics of the oil produced from the Designated area olives that proves also the origin of the oil.

Farms cannot afford to produce olives with the uncertainty of not being accepted for transformations into Designated olive oil. The oil produced with olives from certified plantations cannot be conditioned, rectified, blended or manipulated in any way to be admitted as Protected Designation of Origin. The only intervention allowed is that of adjusting slightly the transformation so that the product can suit better the stringent Protected Designation of Origin standards as Designated for the specific area of production. The transformation is bound to the harvesting by the scheduled time and is a critical activity that cannot be repeated or corrected after its completion. Protected Designation of Origin olive oil is a zero defect product with 'first-time-right' activities.

Quality assurance strategy

The EU quality project of Designated products is updated by agricultural policies, research and dedicated teams of experts in the field of geographical indications and agricultural product style. Regulations and laws are concerned with safety issues for consumers and the public in general and create harmony with positive attributes of products of protected geographical origins. Regulations create a pull of technologies and markets, in the sense that consumers are fundamentally seen as passive entities and the supply chain as an organization that should learn how to produce.

Private initiative is as such guaranteed by law and excess in quality are only destined for the specialty or very upper class market. The EU regulations, although very stringent in the matter of quality, do not provide a bridge between what quality policies actually ask from producers and the research bettering quality throughout the supply chain. Further integration is needed for this purpose between primary activities and the information flowing from support activities devoted to the constant enhancement of quality through research and innovation. This integration requires a constant update to new EU laws that regulate the market and the initiatives of research labs, Universities and research centres that feed information directly to support activities. The integration between quality as prescribed by law and quality as added value by competitive knowledge should happen conjointly to the management and workforce training.

The Protected Designation of Origin olive oil supply chain can embrace strategies in order to reduce losses from production and absorb costs, otherwise attributed to the units produced due to the lack of olives homogeneity and uniformity of olive plantations.

The zero defect strategic approach to quality assurance integrating the EU procedural quality regime seems to be a feasible option open to all job-roles on the supply chain in collaboration with other stakeholders. This should be done in accordance to vision, mission and strategy of the consortium safeguarding the branding and trade mark representing the olive oil. Information flowing from and towards the supply chain is thus transformed in competitive knowledge by research centres and Universities sharing interests in advancing the field of olive oil quality control and researching the role of food in social sciences. Universities are also technological and process change promoters for the olive oil industry and are the best suited for training, knowledge transfer and competitive understanding through innovation. The interaction between the olive oil industry and Universities/research centres should foster relationships that cluster within certain disciplines and sectors like education, customer relationship management and quality control improvement. Education is thus the main cluster in which services for knowledge dissemination fell and from where the upgrade of skills to the new standard of quality systems originates. In fact the same can be said for customer relationship management, involving consumer education to quality and territory appreciation, trust and transparency on quality control procedures.

Zero defect philosophy

Supply chains embrace quality programs as part of a vision strategy. The same is true for olive oil producers and for the whole Protected Designation of Origin olive oil supply chain to improve processes and prevent errors. The zero defect quality philosophy is based on principles that guide the thinking of all job-roles on the supply chain. In practice, it invites operators to think about quality from the early stage of a product lifecycle and to follow it throughout in order to avoid all possible errors in the execution of the activities and achieve savings in terms of time and money on the overall product lifecycle.

The lifecycle starts with the control of plantation quality. Olive trees and soil can be kept in a good agronomic state by following a plan of action suggested by techniques tailored to the particular certified plantation in order to produce first class olives without defects. From the olives checked before harvesting it should be possible to obtain an oil with characteristics sought by the disciplinary of the production area. Modern techniques make it possible to intervene throughout the agronomic season in order to monitor and maintain olive plantations at a high standard. Plantation maintenance and cropping of olives and subsequent transformation in oil are activities tightly connected to each other in terms of time scheduling and constraints aimed at ensuring the right coupling between activities. This is the real first check-point on the chain which marks future outcomes in terms of profit margin. The oils which do not pass Designated testing are downgraded and generally lower in price, whilst all the expenses are added on the final cost of the unit produced.

Transformers are nowadays able to tune pressing systems for high quality output and to satisfy customer requirements. The zero defect philosophy embraces all activities and should not be intended as a practice or a program which can be applied to only some activities. At specified times the primary activities share vital information with the support of the supply chain. Success of the transformation activity is highly dependent on the technology used and precisely, the right type of input is the key determinant of the value added. The quality of oil however, starts in the field and is kept by the olive cropping activity to the highest possible level, by following the correct procedures of harvesting without damaging the fruit and transporting them rapidly in excellent condition to destination.

Prefixed routines of quality control direct each single entry and exit point of job-roles of the chain. Information from activity outcomes should feed support activities which govern the overall quality assurance process and inform each activity required to meet quality standard. An overly mechanistic management view of quality should be discouraged by adopting a more holistic practice in everyday action, in pursuit of excellence.

Intangible qualities

Protected Designation of Origin olive oils take with them intangible qualities which pertain to imaginative experiential and subjective emotional sphere of product consumptions. In fact consumers cannot see the factors which contribute uniquely to the taste and flavours.

The aesthetic experience of appreciation, education, experience sharing and recognition of such characteristics is the added value of a Designated oil. The correlation between sensorial characteristics, origin, natural factors, environmental conditions and human working methods typical of an area, cannot be easily communicated to consumers as such important nuances are intangible even for the expert taster. These nuances become part of the aesthetic experience by appreciating a product, communicating with other consumers the experience of doing so, recounting the moment for reflection and making meaningful moments of oil tasting and consumption for their lives.

The whole experience of consumption cannot be easily divided into well defined parts to be analysed apart from the whole; in the same way it is difficult to unpack consumer experiences into identifiable factors. The quantification of intangible factors may seem to be less realistic than pure quantitative data collected on the supply chain or by customer feedback. Although the quantification is made even more difficult by the evolving nature of consumer decisions as experiential, it should nonetheless be considered as integral part of quality control. This process should be in charge of measuring the intangibility of qualities as they add value and are a determinant differentiation factor, as perceived by consumers, from any other type of Extra Virgin olive oil.

The intangible characteristics not being easily quantifiable, cannot be specified like the tangible one. Consequently it is very difficult to specify requirements for intangible characteristics and even more difficult to know whether these have been met within a coherent quality control plan. Consumers are involved actively as the last ring in the supply chain where sensorial experience starts. Sensory experience is loaded with the embodied values of rural communities, the social-economic development and the reproduction of the physical environment and entropic (culture, local traditions in their various manifestations) food safety and trust for producers. Added value of production for Designated oils is in the typicality of its origin shared by segments of markets in virtues of the provenance from a particular territorial context.

This is the reason why such olive oils are identified with the geographical name of the production area. In this context the geographical name is a sort of synthetic indicator of the product quality and the process involved.

Quantifying intangibility

Management often fails to take seriously those aspects which they consider immeasurable, or that for their very nature are intangible and cannot be quantified with exact measures. In the case of the Designated oil supply chain management, this tendency should be rectified if not avoided.

The first step in balancing the tendency to concentrate on measurable quality factors is to make management, supervisors and job-roles aware of the intangible factors of the product. This can be
achieved not with the typical stand-alone training program but developing a holistic view of their work activities, values, beliefs, connections with the communities of consumers that appreciate their product as integral part of their work. Continuous learning and development of reflective thinking can bridge the distance between consumer perceptions, learning of oil characteristics, experience of consumptions and the working activities on the supply chains.

The working activities of the supply chain become then tangible expressions of social well being, environmentally compatible, highlighting a social sensibility in the appreciation of Designated oils within a lifelong education plan. This decomposition of the intangible qualities of the typical product for a specific area as a Designated oil, finds a correspondence as value created by consumers and as such subject to management observation for improvement.

Quality as determined by intangible factors can then be conveniently seen as a path through which a series of intrinsic and extrinsic characteristics of the oil satisfy consumers.

The exchange of values between supply chain e consumers creates in turn valuable relationships.

Supply chain offers:

Base value of production

Value for conformity

Value for differentiation

Consumer demands:

Value for physical characteristics

Value for intangible characteristics (origin, territory, trust, emotional factors)

Education in quality programs is the sector on which Universities and the

Protected Designation of Origin olive oil industry should constantly entertain relationships as part of new innovation scenarios and to maintain a degree of awareness over quality issues involving consumers in positive experiences in respect of more general lifestyle choices.

Traceability as differentiation

One of the key aspects of the Protected Designation of Origin supply-chain is the responsibility of the job-roles through the operations required by the structures transferring the product and the trust and values put in its production. The supply chain has to reconstruct the history of the product at any time and document all operations and activities. It is duty of the supply chain to follow it up to the final destination. Like other actors in the chain, farmers are directly responsible for their competence and should provide traceability of their operations throughout. Complexity of the relations amongst job-roles on the chain should correspond in a responsible conjoint action through the chain.

Traceability is regulated by law, can represent an opportunity for farmers. Studies have demonstrated that communicating the origin of a product to perspective consumers reduce the perception of risk and stimulate purchase. Systems for consumers to access extensive oil information regarding characteristics, properties and geographical origins, can be strategic tools of competitive advantage. Traceability also covers all contributions given on the supply chain to be accessed as additional information by consumers as a point of differentiation from other products.

Traceability communicates to the consumer, concepts of honesty and transparency and encourages a perception of safety based on evidence of respect of the law. It is an invaluable attribute for a supply chain to stand out in the market with added value based on integrity and transparency for consumers. Traceability creates collective added-value, improving the market position of Designated oils and enhancing collective reputation.

The production of critical quantitative intangible qualities can be traced back to specific oils, becoming part of a program for collective reputations in co-production of individual practices, by informing the community of consumers. Moreover, recognition of origin and quality of oils generates added value in synergy with other products of identified nearby geographical area.

The quality assurance process as established by the procedural legislation of the EU can be a real advantage for the whole chain if relationships amongst various stakeholders are seen in a perspective of collaboration and product differentiation as strategic, overcoming the stall created by branding offering lower quality oils.

There is a complexity of relations behind the origin of products like

Designated oils, that is by first analysing and then valuing such relationships, value can be added on the chain.

Zero defect management

The key driver for quality with the zero-defect practice is the focus on process management. A quality product arises only if the management of a firm, and all of them on the supply chain, will function to achieve quality. Quality defined as conformance to requirements is as such a product of management choices made throughout the supply chain, and communicated to the stakeholders. This will enable the supply chain to work simultaneously and seamlessly towards well fixed objectives. When requirements of a product are fixed and well known from the start the outcomes are achieved in terms of conformance to requirements with zero defects. Such objectives are effectively 'quality' that must be achieved in order to satisfy customer expectations and fulfil the requirements of the EU disciplinary for the product certified as of a very high standard, safe and with known origin traceable at any time.

Quality should be measured however throughout the activities on the supply chain as a building process of continuous evaluation and development, to culminate in the final quality outcome. This is achieved through a stepped approach for quality improvement that relies on a combination of both quantitative and qualitative aspects in harmony with the overall quality program on the supply chain. Such harmony can be achieved only if job-roles on the supply chain are well trained, aware of the quality issues, their costs and are empowered to take action to correct problems and rectify defects or to pass them onto higher supervisory level. The zero defect practice should be planned, job roles should be trained for continuous improvement and manage break-down situations in conformity to an overall quality organizational plan.

Organization managers and supervisors should also be trained on the steps to undertake in the organizational quality improvement program (part of the quality continuous development practice of the supply chain). Zero defect quality is achieved when job-roles receive the right input and obstacles to fulfil their higher performance duties are removed. In fact employees should be given the right tools for obstacles reporting so that they advise management of the factors which prevent them in achieving error-free work. Training for quality the job-roles throughout the supply chain as well as continuous learning for improvement plays a major role in the quality ongoing process for a zero-defect product.

To summarise, the approach to quality suggested for the control of the activities outcomes on the supply chain is centred around three essential strands: Quantification of quality and cost of the defects, management leadership, prevention rather than cure.

The clarity of product requirement remains however a cornerstone with critical impact. In the case of a Designated oil, the requirements are quite straightforward because they are fixed by EU disciplinary and define a physical product. Quality can be quantified through prefixed parameters and certified to consumers by a guarantee of a high quality product.

The guarantee of high quality is certified after a process of quality control which takes a very short time; it is however the whole stepped approach to zero defects as practice of quality enhancement/improvement that can ensure positive results in achieving prefixed quantifiable objectives.

Extending the requirements to encompass intangible qualities is less straightforward, in the sense that these can vary for different Designated oils and can be very dependent on the marketing strategy that a supply chain decide to undertake to promote their oil. Summarily, the type of quantification used to measure intangible qualities and the factors that concur to make such qualities belonging to the oil, should however be well known to the supply chain management, no matter the label or the type of Designated area.

The zero defect management plan proceedes with the involvement of all job-roles on the supply chain in the following four stages running in parallel:

Stage 1

Management commitment

Quality awareness

Training for quality

Defect detection encouragement

Stage 2

Quality teams

Defect correcting

Management training

Removing obstacles to quality

Stage 3

Quality test measurements

Zero defect planning

Train job-roles

Quality councils for improvements

Stage 4

Establish cost of quality

Share zero defect planning

Supply chain harmonization

The meaning of quality

The olive growing industry in Italy has focused in the last years on research and innovation oriented to the development of technology for efficiency transforming olives with very high outputs. Much academic debate has consequently highlighted the fact that an increase in efficiency in the transformation of olives does not correspond necessarily to a higher quality of oil if the fruit does not present quality characteristics. Studies have thus prompted the need for higher agronomic technique standards and quality control for olive growing as a first step in reaching higher quality outcomes.

Olive quality has become a relevant subject for research with advancements in chemistry and in particular into how fatty acids interact to make an olive oil that is of high quality. The supply chain is now requested oils with medical characteristics compatible if not exceeding those suggested by scientific medic research.

The market pull generated by legislation and consumer demand for high quality products, has thus changed the concept of quality, which now involves the whole supply chain indistinctively. Each activity on the supply chain can be supported with specialized research which is becoming as a matter of fact always more integrated. Research outcomes indicate new variable interactions and consequent impact on quality of oils.

Selection of variables and interdisciplinarity of research with other fields is necessary for Designated oils. In fact as food research has advanced in fields like genetics, the olive oil industry has progressed research in fields like genetic traceability, sensorial characterisation, ground conditions that characterise oil, cultivar flavours, working methods that affect the oil quality and flavours. This to satisfy supply chain demands for new research that valorize uniqueness of Designated oils. In synthesis scholars answer questions concerned with «levels of quality» discerning legislative requirements for quality and excellence of olive oils.

Protected Designation of Origin quality is not just «fitness for use» but something unique «valuable» for consumers, producers and the whole chain which brings them into a relationship, including the intentions and the efforts put through production and the values and vision from which they derive. In fact these oils are not just a mix of chemical substances that interact with our senses but also context, labour and effort of production, because these factors are not extraneous to sensory perceptions.

The objectivity of intangible qualities can at this point be summarized as the addition of intangible values which are not part of the physical structure of the oil per se, but in the spirit, in the humanity of who has produced it and in the relations between who consumes it and who has produced it. Honesty, transparency, competence, traceability of products, capacity to improve for efficiency and bettering quality throughout the supply chain are the intangible factors valued by consumers. These factors should be in forms that can be measured and made tangible for management of the supply chain.

Qualities of olive oils are enclosed within four categories encompassing either tangible and intangible factors:

Insufficient

Quality that does not conform to law

Sufficient : All olive oils

Edibility

Excellent: Extra Virgin olive oils

Desirable characteristics sought after by the market

Transparency, medical

Unique: Protected Designation of Origin olive oils

Trust, transparency, authenticity, effort of production

Ability to keep quality as promised

Medical

Origin guarantee

Value creation and product differentiation are thus the main interests for Protected Designation of Origin olive oil research and an area of investment by private and public funding. Such research area cannot be sustained in isolation by small or medium sized olive growers or oil producers, but needs scholarly support and collaboration with academia involvements in all the active phases of the supply chain.

Considerations

A trip to a supermarket or local shop can confirm the wide selection of olive oil for sale. The offer is for customers with the same disposable incom and differences in price are minimal although accommodating also demanding customers with expensive and higher quality oils.

The generous amount of shelf space devoted to olive oils is proof of the positive Mediterranean influence in cooking and the progressive decline of animal fat sales. New blends of olive oils are purchased with confidence by consumers who are increasingly aware of differences in taste. Modern clientele is now able to appreciate a wider spectrum of oil qualities and a new range of tastes.

The Extra Virgin olive oil is however mainly appreciated for cooking at home, whilst the catering industry is making use of a wider selection of brands and higher quality olive oils to satisfy a demanding customer base. Tasting is also a new factor which is giving weight to purchase decisions by more experienced consumers.

Protected Designation of Origin olive oils present subtle nuances in taste and flavour and are purchased following precise criteria of selection, the first being its origin guarantee. Single or blend plantations are another purchase factor for the expert and a referring point for use in cooking or tasting. Hedonic enjoyment is another stimulus to discriminate between choices and an option open to the clientele.

Appreciation of oil taste and flavours is a free life choice not dictated by fashionable statements or occasional branding and promotions. It is a wider interest evolving in a discipline in its own right with various degree of engagement and specializations. Amateur tasters are keen to engage with olive oils for personal interest. Many new to the field are willing to expand their knowledge and enjoy discovering diverse uses of high quality olive oils. Professionals fully engage in activities of guidance and promotions for the higher end market whilst recently, qualified sommeliers have been indicating new directions for appreciation of olive oils combined with food preparation and aesthetics. For this purpose operators on supply chains can establish a knowledgeable network for classifications of oil qualities and experiential aspects of consumption as tool for professional reference and experience sharing. In this sense Designated oils are favoured as choice and logically connected to territory realities.

Oil tasting sessions are opportunities for supply chains to establish relations for exchange and product promotions otherwise difficult to emerge due to high cost of marketing. The opportunity is also open to producers and sole traders willing to engage participants in expanding their interests in oil and access the complexities of intangible qualities. Such events channel naturally new interests and propose moments of knowledge gathering and can be the first point for approaching origin Designated oils.

The catering industry is widening access for new entrants interested in developing their knowledge of taste and flavour for social purpose or as part of free time activities. At the same time marketers should devote attention towards segments of population with more disposable income and in search of stimulus to enjoy free time. Intelligent enjoyment is another value added by expanding knowledge of taste, foods, territory, places and engaging consumers in higher cognitive processes. Intelligent enjoyment for Protected Designation of Origin olive oils consumers is a complement to the visceral enjoyment of oil tasting done per se. This type of engagement establish durable relationships with values exchanged on a deeper level, encouraging the clientele in repeat purchases.

Another development that operators on the supply chain may want to consider is engaging the clientele in such collaborative designs as a starting point that can easily evolve in word-of-mouth for new entrants. This is the best way to get the message across the market with a network of knowledgeable consumers as customer base, saving considerable amounts on marketing costs. The lasting point of collaborative relationships is to provide a durable and reliable tool for supply chains to optimise production, reduce costs, encourage new entrants and assure clientele with the highest quality and forecast sales with precision.

It's superfluous to mention the world wide web as channel to market Designated oils. The reader surely has a presence in the digital marketplace.

The EU Protected Designation of Origin disciplinary documents that describe in full each single designation of olive oil are a reliable source of information for professionals and consumers. Marketers can expand the knowledge base as tool for a standard categorization and professional reference. Finally, such extraordinary oils create a stable and reliable market with demands from the novice to experts, sommeliers, chefs and all interested in living healthily and enjoy life when appreciation means also positive experience and well-being of consumers with guaranteed returns for the whole supply chain.

Bibliography

Allaire, G. (2009) The contribution of geographical indications to rural development
http://economia.unipr.it/de/ecagro/it/food_conference.html
Belletti, G. (2003) Le denominazioni geografiche nel supporto all' agricoltura multifunzionale PAGRI Vol. 4.

Bianchi, G and Giansante, L. (2001) «Tutela degli oli extravergine dop» Industrie agrarie N. 22

Bergman, M.M. (2011) «The good, the bad and the ugly» Journal of Mixed Methods Research Vol. 5, No. 4. pp 271-275

Breznitz, S.M. and Feldman, M.P. (2010) «The engaged university» The Journal of Technology Transfer Vol. 37, No. 2.pp 139-157

Breznitz, S.M. and Feldman, M.P. (2012) «The larger role of the university in economic development: introduction to the special issue» The Journal of Technology Transfer Vol. 37, No. 2. pp 135-138

Brown, J.S. and Duguid, P. (1991), «Organizational Learning and Communities-of-Practice: Toward a Unified View of Working, Learning, and Innovation» Organization Science Vol. 2 No. 1. pp . 40-57

Bryman, A. (2006) «Integrating quantitative and qualitative research: how is it done» Qualitative research Vol. 6, No. 1. pp 97-113

Casieri, A., De Gennaro, B., Cimino, O. and Roselli, L. (2008) Una valutazione degli effetti dell' evoluzione della PAC sul settore, olivicolo. Il caso della Puglia
http://www.depa.unina.it/sidea2008/PAC_settoriali/Casieri_et_al.pdf

Carree, M., Della Malva, A., and Santarelli, E., (2012), « The contribution of Universities to growth: empirical evidence for Italy» The Journal of Technology Transfer Vol. 39, No. 3. pp 393-414

Crosby, P. (1975) Quality is Free McGraw-Hill, New York.

Cruz-Castro, L., Sanz-Menéndez, L., and Martínez, C., (2012), «Research centers in transition: patterns of convergence and diversity» The Journal of Technology Transfer Vol. 37, No. 1. pp 18-42

Daft, L. R. and Weick, E. K. (1984), «Toward a Model of Organisations as Interpretation Systems» Academy of Management Review Vol. 9, No. 2. pp 284-295

De Gennaro, B. and Rosselli, L. (2013) La filiera olivicola-olearia pugliese: struttura, organizzazione e competitività La rivista di scienze dell' alimentazione Vol. 42, No. 1.pp 165-174

Edwin, M.and Jeong-Yeon, L. (1996) «The modern university: contributor to industrial innovation and recipient of industrial R&D support» Research Policy Vol. 25, No. 7. pp 1047-1058

Esposito, M. (2008) Il contesto internazionale dei prodotti a marchio distintivo
http://www.istat.it/it/files/2011/01/esposito.pdf

Fiore, S. (2002) «Designing on-line experience through consideration of the salient sensory attributes of products» Master of Philosophy Thesis, University of Manchester Institute of Science and Technology, England.

Freshwater, D. and Fisher, P. (2014) «(Con) fusing commerce and science: mixed methods research and the production of contextualized knowledge» Journal of Mixed Method Research Vol. 8, No. 2. pp 111-114

Geiger, R.L. (2012) «University supply and corporate demand for academic research» The Journal of Technology Transfer Vol. 37, No. 2. pp 175-191

Grosse Kathoefer, D. and Leker, J. (2012) «Knowledge transfer in academia: an exploratory study on the Not-Invented-Here Syndrome» The Journal of Technology Transfer Vol. 37, No.5. pp 658-675

Husted, K. and Michailova, S. (2002) «Diagnosing and Fighting Knowledge-Sharing Hostility» Organizational Dynamics Vol. 31, No. 1. pp 60-73

Kahlke, R. (2014) «Generic qualitative approaches: pitfalls and benefits of methodological mixology» International Journal of Qualitative Methods Vol. 13, pp. 37-52

ISMEA (2010)   Il mercato delle DOP e IGP in Italia
http://www.ismea.it/flex/cm/pages/ServeBLOB.php/L/IT/IDPagina/3584

Lanza, C.M., Migliori, C. and Mazzaglia, A. (2004) Influenza dei sistemi estrattivi sulle caratteristiche qualitative degli oli DOP Industrie alimentari   No. XLIII

Mangialardi, P. (2011) Agriturismo e ospitalità rurale Hoepli, Milan.

Mannina, L., Patumi, M., Proietti, N. and A.L. Segre, (2001) «PDO: Geographical characterization of Tuscan extra virgin olive oil using high field HNMR spectroscopy» Italian Journal of Food Science Vol. 13, No. 1. pp 53-63

Marchini, A. and Diotallevi, F. (2010) Analisi di competitività degli oli di extravergine di oliva nel canale della GDO
http://ssrn.com/abstract=2185680

Nonaka, I. (1994) «A dynamic theory of organisational knowledge creation» Organization Science Vol. 5, No.1. pp 14-31

Peri, C. (2008) Eccellenza dell' olio d' oliva Edizioni Polistampa, Firenze.

Perkman, M. and Walsh, K. (2007) «University-Industry relationships and open innovation: Towards a research agenda" International Journal of Management Review Vol. 9, No. 4. pp 259-280

Porter, M. (1985) Competitive advantage Free Press.

Roselli, L., Casieri, A., De Gennaro, B. and Medicamento, U. (2013) Olive oils protected by EU geographical indications: creation and distribution of the value-adding within supply chains http://ageconsearch.umn.edu/bitstream/58125/2/Roselli.pdf.

Servili M., De Stefano, G., Piacquadio, P., Di Giovacchino, L. and Sciancalepore, V. (1999) «Effect of extraction systems on the phenolic composition of virgin olive oils» European Journal Of Lipid Science And Technology No. 101 pp 328-332

'Shea et al, O. (2005) «Entrepreneurial orientation, technology transfer and spinoff performance» Research Policy Vol. 34, No. 7. pp 994-1009

Tsimidou, M. (1998) «Polyphenols and quality of virgin olive oil in retrospect» Italian Journal of Food Science Vol. 10, No. 2. pp 99–11

Visioli, F. (2008) «Olio d' Oliva: gli aspetti salutistici» pp 71-77 in Accademia dei Georgofili L'olivo ed il suo olio Edizioni Polistampa, Florence.

About the author

Salvatore Fiore has worked in Italy as computer programmer and system analyst for the optical reading industry before studying information business and management at Brunel University in the UK receiving subsequently an Honours degree from the Open University. He has also received a M.Phil. in Computation from the University of Manchester in 2002, discussing a thesis on online sale of fresh produce.

The growing interest for the "dots com" has determined a new line of confrontation for the business of fresh produce. Product attributes cannot be easily represented at the interface, thus deterring investments by grocers on digital markets. The online grocery business is however more convincing when confronting the impressive amount of money invested in local shops with negative income statements. The computer interface, is seen then less problematic and standardization of supply chains, trust, convenience and delivery of quality on the promise prevail.

Salvatore Fiore has postulated and demonstrated that the interaction by potential online customers of fresh produce can approximate to physical interaction as carried out in a brick-and-mortar shop.

He has recently researched the olive growing industry and the production system with certified origins in Puglia (South Italy). The Protected Designation of Origin is a EU standard protected by law with bodies which regulate the disciplinary of production for Designated products. Salvatore Fiore is currently studying the certification system and future implications for the olive oil industry and developments in education for the supply chain management of Designated olive oils.

The work presented in this book is part of the dissertation analysis presented for the Masters in Business Administration Education at Keele University, UK. The dissertation investigates the role of Universities supporting the Designated oil "Terre Tarentine".

The Masters thesis postulates that olive growers, producers and bottlers cannot sustain the complexities of the olive oil market for Designated areas of production in Taranto Boroughs without the support of scholarly, University education and partnerships for knowledge transfer. Company size, competence and lack of resources for investments in areas outside the EU agricultural and rural planning, are the major factors in deterring small-medium size companies in embracing Product Designation of Origin as a standard production model. The University of Keele awarded Salvatore Fiore the MBA Education in 2015.

Salvatore Fiore is an olive grower and a fully qualified oil sommelier engaged in continuous education for olive oil studies and environmental issues.

www.ingramcontent.com/pod-product-compliance
Lightning Source LLC
Chambersburg PA
CBHW051212220526
45473CB00003B/1000